With You As My Friend

Thoughts for a Very Special Person

Paula Finn

Bristol Park Books

First Bristol Park Books edition published in 2017

Bristol Park Books
252 West 38th Street
New York, NY 10018

Bristol Park Books is a registered trademark
of Bristol Park Books, Inc.

Library of Congress Control Number:2017938928

ISBN:978-0-88486-657-2

E-Book ISBN:978-0-88486-658-9

Text and cover design by Keira McGuinness
Cover art copyright © 2017 Jung Suk Hyun/Shutterstock

Printed in Malaysia

Everyone has a friend they can call special—but few are blessed with one as special…as the friend I have in you.

To

_____

From

_____

The
Friend
I Have
In You

On the day I first met you,

I received the gift of companionship—

the pleasure of long walks and heartfelt talks

with someone who understands me deeply,

and accepts me just the way I am...

the gift of strength to help me defeat my fears or fatigue...

of support to make my triumphs mean more,

and my losses hurt less... of comfort

   to soften my deepest pain...

of inspiration to lift me from my darkest mood.

On the day I first met you, I received the gift of friendship

And that has made every day since then

...so much more beautiful.

You

Recognize

The Best

In Me

Friend...

You recognize the best in me
   and help me to express it.

I can share with you equally
my success and failure
   for I know that neither will be judged.

You take time to hear
my everyday problems
   and sincerely care that they are solved.

My concerns are important to you
because they are important to me.
   And you always make me feel worthwhile.

I can think of no higher ambition
than to be for someone
as great a friend
    as you have been for me.

Our friendship was just beginning...
when already it seemed as though
we'd known each other forever.
It felt so natural to share
our interests and adventures,
to confide faults and celebrate strengths,
to be ourselves—

in the security of each other's

warmth and acceptance...

Our friendship was just beginning,

when already I cared very much about you...

I wanted to share in the events of your day—

to hear your good news and bad,

to enhance your joys

and help you grow from your sorrows.

I wanted you to have the best—

 and I wanted to help you achieve it...

Our friendship was just beginning,

when already I trusted you completely

to listen without judging,

to forgive without blaming,

to be honest without hurting,

to give what I needed...

and to accept what I needed to give.

Our friendship was just beginning,

when already I knew...

that it would never end.

You've Been

A True

Friend

To Me

You've Been a True Friend to Me

Lately I've been thinking
of how much you have given me,
and how little I have thanked you...

for always being there
to provide a listening ear
and a helping hand,
whether my problem is large or small...

for supporting me equally
through my achievements
and my setbacks—
for accepting all that I am,
while inspiring me to be more...

for giving so freely of your time
and your self...
for showing me
that my thoughts and feelings
are important to you,
and my companionship is welcome...

for encouraging me to let go of old fears
and to move on toward new goals—
for believing so steadily in my dreams,
and helping me find the courage
to reach them...

for setting an example
of what I would most like to be—
a person who speaks from the heart
and listens with the soul...
a person who cares.

You've been a true friend to me.
Your kindness is something
I can never repay
—and something I will never forget.

No

One

But

You

No One But You...

No one could ever make me laugh
as easily as you,
or restore my perspective so quickly
when the sun has disappeared
from my day...

No one could understand me
as deeply as you,
by interpreting my words as I mean them,
sensing my unspoken thoughts,
or sharing my most private emotions...

No one could make me feel
as special as you,
by taking a sincere interest
in what I think, say and feel;
by always being ready
to give me the time I need,
and to appreciate the time I give...

No one could support me
as completely as you,
by sharing my sorrows as readily
as my joys;
by accepting what I am—
    and loving me for it.

No one could be a better friend to me
than you...
and no one could appreciate you
    more than I.

I'm
Thankful For
Every Day
We're Friends

I'm Thankful for Every Day We're Friends

This isn't a holiday or special occasion,
but it is a good day for me
to acknowledge the ways
you make my life easier,
happier...and so much richer.

It's such a comfort to share with you
the good and bad things I go through—
knowing you'll be there
to understand my fears
and validate my feelings
helps me believe I can cope
with any difficulty I might face.

So often my triumphs have become your joys,
and my losses have brought you sorrow;
you've worried with me
through my most difficult problems,
and shared my relief when they were solved.

Talking with you always gives me
a clearer perspective.
You keep me from getting upset
over the things that aren't important—
and you share my concern
    for the things that are...

From your spirit and support
I draw new enthusiasm for my passions,
new confidence in my dreams,
and new tolerance for others—
and for myself.

Whatever my needs,
you make every effort to
    give your best—
your most thoughtful attention,
most helpful advice,
and most generous support.
You make every effort...
    to make a difference.

And while this isn't a holiday,
it still is very special—
for I've come to see that any day
that we are friends
...is a day for me to celebrate.

The strength of our friendship
is honesty...
We're not afraid or ashamed
to reveal our true thoughts
and to express our innermost feelings.
We tell each other the truth
although it may hurt,

for we know that telling a lie
would hurt us even more.

The comfort of our friendship
is acceptance...
We celebrate the best in each other
while forgiving the flawed.
Through wins and losses,
good moods and bad—
what we give is appreciated;
who we are is enough...
The spirit of our friendship
is love...

An abundant source
of warmth and pleasure
that gives special meaning
to everything we share—
a love that will forever
be counted among
my life's greatest
blessings.

The beauty of
our friendship
...is you.

With You

As

My Friend

With You as My Friend...

I enjoy the warmth
of truly caring for someone
   and of being cared for,
the confirmation
that my ideas and opinions
   are valid—and valued,
the ease
of being understood
   without having to explain,
the satisfaction
   of feeling needed,
and the freedom to express myself openly
   without being judged.

With you as my friend,

I enjoy the comfort of knowing

I'll always have...

a shoulder to lean on,

a hand to reach out for...

and a heart to

welcome me

home.

Thank You
For
Being There

Thank You for Being There

You hear my dreams and you inspire me.
You sense my doubts and you encourage me.
You watch my growth and you applaud me.

You feel my pain
and you support me.

You know my faults
and you accept me.

Thank you for being there
   when I need you...
Thank you for being the friend that you are.

As

Your

Friend

As Your Friend...

I encourage you to pursue the interests
you're passionate about,
to learn the things you're curious about,
and to live the life you dream about.
I want you to do whatever you need
...to be happy.

I'm on your side.
My caring for you is sincere,
my faith in you is strong,
and my support for you is complete.
I respect your choices,
whether or not I would make them;
I welcome your opinions,

whether or not I can share them...

I worry about your problems,

I mourn your losses,

and I celebrate your triumphs.

Whatever is important to you ...is important to me.

As your friend,

I appreciate your best,

and I forgive your flaws.

I'm not here to criticize, pressure,

or try to change you—

for you can only be what you are.

And what you are...is beautiful.

I'm Proud
To Be
Your Friend

I'm Proud To Be Your Friend

You're one of those rare persons
who lives up to,
and goes beyond

my idea of what a true friend should be...
someone who not only makes promises,
but keeps them...
who not only thinks of nice things to do
—but does them.

You listen with an open mind,
and respond from the heart...
your feedback is honest and insightful.
You take the time to give your best...
You take the time to care.

Through all my upsets and uncertainties,

you've been my one constant source

of strength—

easing my worries,

inspiring my dreams...

and investing your time,

energy, and your heart

   into helping me achieve them...

You see the sun through the clouds,
and you look for the good in bad experiences.
You can find a bright side
to the most difficult situation...
and you inspire me to do the same.

Thinking of the beauty you add to my life
makes me realize
how lucky I am that you are my friend...
and how proud I am to be yours.

Your

Friendship

Has Made

All The Difference

Your Friendship Has Made All The Difference

Your kindness has helped me
to admit my mistakes,
and to forget them...

your support has led me
to face my fears,
and to defeat them...
your faith has inspired me
to expect good things
—and to find them.

In a lifetime,
I could never repay you for the gifts
that have made my cloudiest days sunny,

and my brightest dreams real...
gifts that came at just the right time,
in just the right way—
shared so unselfishly
from the best of your wisdom,
the richness of your spirit...
and the depth of your heart.

Whenever I have a problem,
I know I can draw
on your strength and compassion
to help me cope...

Your willingness to offer suggestions
or simply to listen—
makes it easier for me to think,
to sort through my confusion, and to get in touch
with what really feels right.

You always understand.
Even through my most difficult days
and my strangest moods,
you know how I could say what I say
and why I act as I do.
You look behind my words
to appreciate their deeper meanings,
sensing what's on my mind...
and hearing what's in my heart.

You provide a safe place where I can relax, reflect,
and renew my desire to face the world again.
With you, I never have to be anything more
or anything less than what I honestly am—
my smallest gifts are appreciated,
and my biggest mistakes are forgiven.

You've known me as I've soared
and as I've stumbled—
yet through all the ups and downs,
your faith in me has been strong,
your concern has been genuine,
and your support has been constant.

Indeed, You give new meaning
to the word "friend."

A
Friend
Like
You

A Friend Like You...

Good times seem even better

when I enjoy them with you...

you're fun to be around,

and you make it easy to laugh.

It makes you happy

to see me happy,

and it means a lot

to know I can count on you

to celebrate my triumphs

and share in my joys

as though they were your own.

Dear friend,

it means even more to know

you'll be with me
through my rough times as well—
that I'll have your concern
and your willingness to accept my tears,
to share my pain,
and be the one person
who keeps me from feeling alone.

I know that no storm lasts forever—
the sun will always return
to shine even brighter than before...

and I will emerge from any of life's difficulties

even stronger than before...

I have courage and stamina,

and most important,

a friend like you...

to stand by me until I do.

Our

Times

Together

Our Times Together

Together we talked...
Together we listened...
Together we grew.

Your laughter warmed me
through many winters...
Your tears nourished me
through many sorrows.

Our times together,
meaningful in their simplicity,
will remain a profound gift to my life.

Thank you for the experience of your friendship.

The More I Know You

The More I Know You...

the more I realize how generous you are.

You've always made the time

and found the energy

to graciously welcome me

into your busiest day...

to give me your full attention,

to acknowledge my concerns

as important,

my opinions as valid,

and my dreams as possible,

to offer your best resources,

your wisest advice,

and your fullest support.

Whatever my needs,

I know that you care...

from the concern I see in your eyes,

the warmth I hear in your voice...

and the goodness I feel in your soul...

The more I know you...

the more I appreciate your kindness.

You care about how your words affect me,

and you have never said anything

tactless or hurtful.

You never take me for granted,

ignore my needs,

or in any way try

to diminish my self-esteem.

The more I know you...
the more I enjoy your company.
I find things funny with you
that I'd never laugh at by myself;
I enjoy everyday pastimes
I'd never have fun at alone.
Whatever we do together,
the time always flies by—
it doesn't take a special occasion
for us to have a special time.

The more I know you...
the more thankful I am
...that I do!

Everyone

Needs

Someone

Everyone needs someone...

to believe in their dreams,

and to stand behind them in their struggle

to achieve them,

no matter how long,

or how rocky that road proves to be...

to cheer their wins

and to cushion their falls;

to touch their heart

and to reach their soul...

to see them as they are,

while inspiring them to be more...

to be their comfort when they hurt,
their guidance when they stumble,
their stability
when the world or their life
     move too fast...

to take them seriously—
to laugh at their jokes
and cry for their sorrows;
to commend their efforts
and consider their ideas...

to be their most loyal companion,
their closest confidant,
and their best friend...

to make them feel special,
appreciated, and loved.

Everyone needs someone...

Thank you for being
someone I can need.

The more time that passes,
the more I appreciate
the enduring depth and comfort
of our connection.

Through the years, we have nurtured each other,

challenged each other,

and changed each other

in ways too profound to measure.

We realize that the strongest friendships

requires an ability to give

and to receive,

to talk

and to listen...

to be strong enough

for the other person to lean on us

and secure enough

to let ourselves lean on them...

to keep things in perspective:
to cherish the good times,
and ride out the rough times...
to ease tensions with humor,
handle mishaps with grace,
and heal hurts with love...

to be there in the sunshine
and just as available through the rain;
to share in the other person's laughter
and be comfortable with their tears;
to accept them as they are today
...and to support them as they grow.

Dearest friend,
I hope you realize
how thankful I am for our friendship...
and how committed I am
   to making it last forever.

Thank You
For Your Gentle
Words

Thank you

for your gentle words,

your warm thoughts,

your kind deeds...

And most of all,

　your precious friendship.

The beauty of our friendship

is that it is based on respect.

The joy of our friendship is that it is based on trust.

The strength of our friendship

is that it is based on...Love.

Your willingness to stand behind me

through all my life's challenges

has freed me to take the risks

and face the fears

that had long stood in the way

of my dreams...

to dig deeper

and to reach higher,

knowing you would strengthen me

if I weakened—

...and you would catch me if I fell.

Your understanding of me

helps me feel that I'm not alone in the world—

You know my strengths,
   and how they have served me...
you know my faults,
   and what they have cost me;
you know my passions,
   and how much I enjoy them...
you know my losses,
   and how much I mourn them.

You make me feel safe
by being so gentle when I'm weak,
so patient when I struggle,
and so solid and steady,
no matter how fast my life moves.

Your energy inspires me, whatever I do—
Your caring warms me, wherever I am.
We don't have to talk regularly
for our connection to influence
my mood and well-being.

Just knowing you're there...
^...makes all the difference.

I

Admire

Your

Positivity

I admire your positivity

I'm often surprised by how much fun

ordinary activities are

when we do them together.

You bring an energy and humor to everyday things

that makes them seem special;

you've opened my mind to experiences I'd never known;

you've opened my eyes to beauty I'd never seen.

No matter how big a mistake I've made,

or how disappointing a loss I've suffered,

talking with you always helps me

to change my outlook on it—

to feel better about who I am

...and more thankful for what I have.

I can trust you to always be

the person I think you are.

You don't ever play games

or hide your true self—

your smile for me is genuine...

your tears for me are real.

If you're unhappy about something I've done,

you tell me—

and you work with me until we resolve it.

Our communication is open, direct,

and healthy.

I look forward to a forever friendship between us—

And with each day, I'll be celebrating you—

for the goodness,

warmth, and giving that add so much

beauty to our friendship...and

bring so much joy to my life.

Our

Mutual

Support

Our mutual support

It makes it easier
to face any hardship,
carry any weight,
overcome any fear,
...and reach any dream.

At times we've challenged each other,
defied each other,
and even
angered each other,
but we both recognize
that conflict is a natural part of caring.

We see each other as equals,
appreciating the differences between us...
and sharing a mutual respect
for each other's beliefs,
tolerance for each other's faults...
and recognition of each other's strengths.

Together, we've built an enduring connection
of strength and support
that makes our problems look smaller,
our hopes shine brighter,
...and our joys feel deeper,
that enhances the good times,
eases the sad times,
and survives the rough times—

a connection that nourishes us,
despite the miles that lie between;
and grows stronger,
despite the years that pass.

And while I chose this particular day to tell you,
there isn't a day that these words
wouldn't be true...
For there isn't a day that I don't appreciate
your loyal compassion and caring,
—and thank you deeply
for your presence in my life.

Illustration Credits